SEA OTTERS

by Jaclyn Jaycox

PEBBLE
a capstone imprint

Published by Pebble, an imprint of Capstone
1710 Roe Crest Drive, North Mankato, Minnesota 56003
capstonepub.com

Library of Congress Cataloging-in-Publication Data
Names: Jaycox, Jaclyn, 1983– author.
Title: Sea otters / by Jaclyn Jaycox.
Description: North Mankato, Minnesota : Pebble, [2022] | Series: Animals | Includes bibliographical references and index. | Audience: Ages 5–8 | Audience: Grades K–1 | Summary: "There are 13 different kinds of otters. But sea otters are the only kind that spends their whole lives in water! Easy-to-read text and vibrant photos will capture reader's interest to learn all they can about these cute mammals."— Provided by publisher.
Identifiers: LCCN 2021029761 (print) | LCCN 2021029762 (ebook) | ISBN 9781663971760 (hardcover) | ISBN 9781666325232 (paperback) | ISBN 9781666325249 (pdf) | ISBN 9781666325263 (kindle edition)
Subjects: LCSH: Sea otter—Juvenile literature.
Classification: LCC QL737.C25 J39 2022 (print) | LCC QL737.C25 (ebook) | DDC 599.769/5—dc23
LC record available at https://lccn.loc.gov/2021029761
LC ebook record available at https://lccn.loc.gov/2021029762

Image Credits
Alamy: Richard Mittleman/Gon2Foto, 24; Newscom: Danita Delimont Photography/Jim Goldstein, 13, Danita Delimont Photography/Jon Cornforth, 10, Design Pics/Milo Burcham, 11, Harry M. Walker, 27, Minden Pictures/Michio Hoshino, 21, Minden Pictures/Norbert Wu, 17, Minden Pictures/Suzi Eszterhas, 7; Science Source: Thomas Pat Leeson, 19; Shutterstock: cybercrisi, 25, Marco Rimola, 14, Menno Schaefer, 15, Neil Aronson, Cover, Santiparp Wattanaporn, 12, Scenic Corner, 23, Sean Lema, 5, Tory Kallman, 9, VisionDrive, 26, Waridsara_HappyChildren, 28, worldwildlifewonders, 22

Editorial Credits
Editors: Gena Chester and Abby Huff; Designer: Dina Her; Media Researcher: Jo Miller; Production Specialist: Tori Abraham

All internet sites appearing in back matter were available and accurate when this book was sent to press.

Table of Contents

Words in **bold** are in the glossary.

Amazing Sea Otters

Look! There's a cute and furry animal. It's floating in the ocean. What could it be? It's a sea otter!

Sea otters are a kind of **marine mammal**. They live in the water. But they breathe air. They give birth to live young. They have fur. There are 13 kinds of otters. But only sea otters can spend their whole lives in the water.

Where in the World

There are three kinds of sea otters. All are found in the Pacific Ocean. Southern sea otters live close to California. Northern sea otters are found near Alaska and Washington. Russian sea otters live around Russia and Japan.

Sea Otter Range Map

North America

Europe

Asia

Atlantic Ocean

Pacific Ocean

Pacific Ocean

Africa

South America

Indian Ocean

Australia

Range

N
W ⬌ E
S

Southern Ocean

Antarctica

Sea otters don't often go on land. But they stay close by. They usually live within 0.6 miles (1 kilometer) of the shore.

Sea otters don't have nests or burrows. Instead, they live near kelp forests. Kelp is tall seaweed. It grows up from the ocean floor. Sea otters may wrap up in kelp when they rest. This keeps them from floating out into the ocean.

kelp

Sea Otter Bodies

No other animal has fur as thick as sea otters. They have about 1 million hairs per square inch (6.5 square centimeters). That is a lot of fur! A cat only has about 600,000 hairs on its whole body.

Sea otters have two layers of fur. The undercoat is usually dark brown. The longer top layer can be black or brown. Older otters may have silver fur on their heads.

webbed feet

Sea otters spend most of their time floating. They lay on their backs. Their back feet are **webbed**. This helps them push through the water. They use their flat tails to **steer**.

Sea otters live in cold water. Their fur keeps them warm. It is waterproof. It traps heat next to their skin. Being dirty can damage the fur. So sea otters spend hours cleaning it.

A sea otter cleans its fur.

Sea otters are one of the smallest marine mammals. They can grow to almost 5 feet (1.5 meters) long. They can weigh up to 100 pounds (45 kilograms). They have long bodies. Their heads are small and wide.

Sea otters have a great sense of smell. They have good eyesight too. But it can be hard to see through thick seaweed. A sea otter's whiskers sense **vibrations**. This helps it find food.

On the Menu

A sea otter dives to the ocean floor. It spots a tasty crab. It grabs the **prey** with its front paws. It swims back to the surface. Time to eat!

Sea otters eat many sea creatures. They make meals of clams, crabs, and snails. They eat small, spiny animals called sea urchins too. Some also eat fish and small octopuses.

A sea otter cracks open a sea urchin.

Sea otters use rocks as tools to help them eat clams and other prey.

Sea otters dive underwater to catch prey. They can hold their breath for up to five minutes. Their strong paws can flip over big rocks. They look for food hiding on the ocean floor.

Sea otters use tools. They are one of the few mammals that do. They use rocks to crack open shells of prey. They save the rocks for later. They keep them in loose skin in their armpits.

Life of a Sea Otter

Sea otters live in groups called rafts. A raft can have two sea otters. Or it can have up to 1,000! Rafts are usually all males or all females. The sea otters may hold paws while they sleep. This keeps them from floating apart.

Males and females come together to **mate**. Females carry their babies for four to five months. They usually give birth to one baby at a time. Baby sea otters are called pups.

A newborn pup weighs 3 to 5 pounds (1.4 to 2.3 kg). The pup is born with very thick fur. The fur traps a lot of air. This makes the pup float.

The mother cares for the pup. She keeps it clean. It rides on her stomach. It drinks her milk.

When the mother needs to hunt, the pup stays at the surface. She wraps it in kelp. This keeps the pup from floating away in the ocean.

Pups still drink milk while they learn to hunt.

A pup grows adult fur after about two to three months. It loses its baby fur. Then it can dive with its mother. It learns how to hunt. The pup stops drinking milk after about eight months. Then it leaves its mother.

After about four years, sea otters are adults. They are ready to have pups of their own. They can live up to 20 years.

Dangers to Sea Otters

Sea otters have a number of **predators**. Orcas and great white sharks eat sea otters. Bears hunt them too. Bald eagles can snatch pups.

Sea otters swim from danger. Or they hide in seaweed. Some even go on land to get away from predators.

great white shark

A sea otter raft near California

Humans are a danger to sea otters too. Sea otters can get caught in fishing nets. Oil spills can ruin their waterproof fur. **Polluted** water can make them sick.

People used to hunt sea otters. They sold their fur. Sea otters almost became **extinct**. Laws keep them safe now. Their numbers have come up some. But they are still in danger.

You can do things to help sea otters. Recycle. Pick up trash and toss it in garbage cans. Trash on the ground can end up in the ocean.

Fast Facts

Name: sea otter

Habitat: ocean, near kelp forests and not far from land

Where in the World: Pacific Ocean

Food: clams, crabs, snails, sea urchins, fish, octopuses

Predators: orcas, great white sharks, bears, bald eagles

Life Span: up to 20 years

Glossary

extinct (ik-STINGKT)—no longer living; an extinct animal is one that has died out

marine mammal (muh-REEN MAM-uhl)—a mammal that lives in water; a mammal is a warm-blooded animal that breathes air and usually has hair or fur; female mammals feed milk to their young

mate (MEYT)—to join with another to produce young

polluted (puh-LOO-ted)—filled with harmful materials that hurt living things

predator (PRED-uh-tur)—an animal that hunts other animals for food

prey (PRAY)—an animal hunted by another animal for food

steer (STEER)—to move or guide in a certain direction

vibration (vahy-BREY-shuhn)—a fast movement back and forth

webbed (WEHBD)—having folded skin or tissue between the toes or fingers

Read More

Borgert-Spaniol, Megan. *Sea Otters: Kelp Forest Keepers*. Minneapolis: Abdo Publishing, 2020.

McConnell, Cathleen. *Otters: River or Sea?: A Compare and Contrast Book*. Mt. Pleasant, SC: Arbordale Publishing, LLC, 2021.

Schuh, Mari. *Sea Otters*. Minneapolis: Jump!, Inc., 2021.

Internet Sites

National Geographic Kids: Sea Otter
kids.nationalgeographic.com/animals/mammals/facts/sea-otter

SeaOtters.com: Sea Otter Facts
seaotters.com

The Kids Should See This: The Fantastic Fur of Sea Otters
thekidshouldseethis.com/post/deep-look-the-fantastic-fur-of-sea-otters

Index

About the Author

Jaclyn Jaycox is a children's book author and editor. She lives in southern Minnesota with her husband, two kids, and a spunky goldendoodle.